Dear Flynn,

I am so happy to share Lola with you! I hope you enjoy the little puppy that I picked just for you! I hope I get to meet you one day!

Love,
(Author) Essie

"We're all in this together!
Love,
Lola

Lola,
the Roving Reporter

Lola,
the Roving Reporter

A 'Tail' of LOVE

WRITTEN BY
Essie Laflamme

ILLUSTRATED BY
Marie Crane Yvon

Sweet Echo Stories

Printed in China

Design consultant John Balkwill

This book is available from our
Sweet Echo Stories website,
Amazon, and locally owned bookstores.

Sweet Echo Stories

sweetechostories.com

A Bark is Worth a Thousand Words

To every child who cares for, respects and loves all furry friends. Thank you for walking us, playing with us and for your unconditional love. I wag my tail and raise my paw to you!

To every insect, bird or animal (especially you squirrels), that I am privileged to call my friends.

I smell and love you all.

 Love,
Lola

P.S. I am also grateful for balls and treats!

Ready or Not!

Once upon a time, on one warm summer day, a puppy was born.

All the animals, birds and bugs in the happy town of Peaceville were thrilled!

One by one they hopped, jiggled, flew and wiggled over to meet and celebrate their new pal, Lola.

They brought treats, balls and chew toys to welcome their new friend.

Lola greeted each morning with a stretch, a rollover and a hunt for her ball. Then she'd bounce out the door.

Lola's hobby soon became roaming around town asking everyone she met how their day was smelling. At times her pals found this annoying, but mostly they were grateful she had the gift of sniff.

Everyone in Peaceville worked and played and cared for each other. Lola's pals would smile and say, "The only way to have a good friend is to be a good friend!"

Lola loved hearing those words and would joyfully wag her tail and bark,

"We're all in this together!"

Her friends marveled at how Lola would show up just at the right time if something was lost or if someone needed help.

If her dog pals lost their ball, Lola would sniff it out and find it for them.

If a couple of squirrels were hunting for acorns, Lola would sniff out the best tree with the most acorns in it.

If her raccoon pals needed a snack, Lola would sniff out the best trash cans.

If Farmer Rabbit needed help in his garden, Lola would sniff out the best dirt and help him plant carrots.

Day after happy day, Lola frolicked around Peaceville with her nose into every bit of news.

Her friends told her because of her amazing sniffing skills, she should become their "Roving Reporter!" Lola barked, "Hot diggity dog!" Reporting the news soon became her full time job!

For Lola, this work was love at first bark.

With pen in hand
she began to write
her Nose Reports.

"We're all in this together! Arf!"

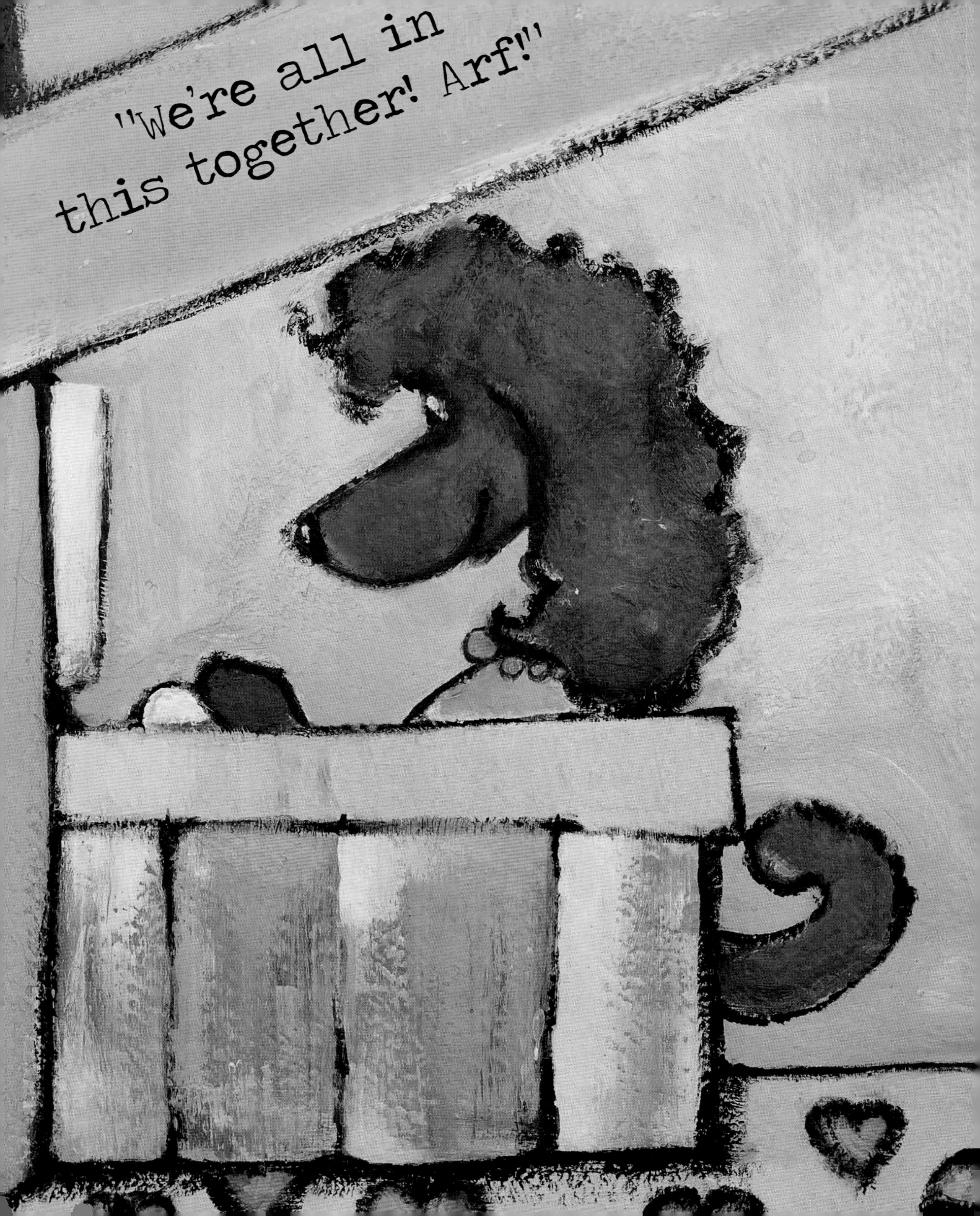

Lola's pals helped her build a desk in her cozy dog house. Her friends loved hearing their news. While she was busy roaming they would happily shout, "Hey Lola, you're top dog! What's the good word today?" Lola would laugh and woof, "I'll let you know later on. Stay tuned!"

At the end of every day, Lola reported the good news throughout Peaceville. "Lola, the Roving Reporter" was a hit!

Lola's happy Nose Reports continued for a very long time. Things seemed like they would always stay this way. Until . . .

Gradually, Lola began to notice some big changes in Peaceville. With her gift of sniff, she started picking up a different smell - and it wasn't good! What was once their bright and happy town was beginning to look like the town dump!

Lola sniffed out smelly trash that had been thrown on neighbors' lawns. She saw gardens that had been trampled on.

Most of all, she heard loud bickering everywhere. There was no ignoring this any longer!

After observing all this chaos Lola knew she had to share the news. She headed back to her dog house to deliver her Nose Report.

"Good evening my friends, tonight my usual good news is not so good. Today. . .

In the park, a huge acorn fight was taking place between two squirrels accusing the other of stealing each other's nuts.

In a nearby backyard, two dogs were loudly growling, accusing each other of digging a huge hole which several animals kept falling into.

In a big tree overhead, two crows loudly cawed in laughter as they poked fun at the animals that kept falling into that hole.

In the yard next door, two raccoons were seen throwing trash at each other and chuckling as they knocked down several cans along their path.

In a nearby garden, a bunny was
on the loose after stealing a
bunch of carrots from an older
rabbit who had trouble hopping.
The bunny was heard laughing
and yelling,

I got away with it!"

"What to do?"

Lola finished her report, and just before curling up to sleep, she wondered, "How can we bring back our good news?" Lola rolled over and softly woofed, "I know my pals and they'll figure it out."

Next morning at dawn, Lola sent out a special report. She sent a message to all her friends asking them to stop their arguing and meet at her dog house.

She told them to bring brooms, wheelbarrows and trash bags.

Her pals were quite concerned. They even stopped arguing with one another for the first time in a very long time. When they knocked on her front door, much to their surprise, Lola wasn't there! Lola was always where she said she would be! They couldn't believe it!

They checked the fire hydrants. No Lola. They checked the grassy hilltop where Lola napped. No Lola. They checked the park. No Lola. As they rounded the last corner they suddenly stopped.

There, in the middle of the trash, was Lola! Lola didn't look up at them. She just continued sweeping, filling up holes and picking up trash. Her pals looked around and, one by one, they began to help.

They smiled and reminded each other, "The only way to have a good friend is to be a good friend!"

They quietly began sweeping along with Lola, picking up trash and making their town bright and happy, just like it used to be.

The best part is, while they worked, they started to whistle and laugh, just like they always had!

This was exactly what Lola had hoped for! Once again, not only did their little world look good, it smelled good, too!

After they finished cleaning up the mess in Peaceville, they went back to Lola's dog house and threw the best party ever!

The raccoons, dogs and squirrels provided the music. The ants came marching in with cookie crumbs for all. The rabbits brought carrot cake and the crows gave free lifts to everyone at the end of the night.

Singing, dancing and laughter could be heard everywhere. The peace was back in their happy town!

That evening, after all of her friends had gone home, Lola shared her Nose Report.

"Good evening my friends. Today is filled with good news! Today was about working and playing and caring for one another! Job well done!"

Lola barked with joy as she ended with her favorite words,

"We're all in this together!"

Lola turned on her nightlight and, just before curling up to sleep, she wondered, "How can we keep this good news going?" Lola closed her eyes and softly woofed, "I know my pals and they'll figure it out."

The next morning Lola woke up and was startled to see her ant pals staring at her. They told her to check her messages. Lola smiled the biggest smile as she began to read.

The first message came from the squirrels.

"Dear Lola, we've decided to work together to find acorns and share them with the older squirrels who can't climb trees anymore! We figured out that not helping others is just plain nuts!"

The next report was from the dogs.

"Hi Lola, all of us dogs have such remarkable digging skills that we've decided that after digging holes we will put our paws together and fill them back up. That way nobody gets hurt. Arf!"

The crows wrote, "Hi Lola, sorry for cackling at the animals for falling in those holes! The other day we were laughing so hard at them that we flew into a tree! We know that making fun isn't funny! From now on if anyone falls into a hole, we will be happy to fly them out of it!"

The raccoons chimed in. "You know Lola, the reason we knock down trash cans is because we're always hungry. We are really sorry. We've decided to pick up the trash everyday and no longer throw it at each other."

Bunny's message was next. "Dear Lola, please tell Farmer Rabbit I'm sorry I've been taking carrots from his garden. The truth is, I don't know how to grow my own."

Lola smiled because just after that message Farmer Rabbit wrote, "I was once a little bunny. I didn't know how to garden. An older rabbit taught me and now I would like to teach bunny how to grow her very own carrots!"

Now this was more like it! Lola celebrated by taking a trot around town. Lola gave each pal her paw, thanking them for bringing the peace back to Peaceville.

That night everyone gathered around to listen to Lola's happy Nose Report:
"Good evening good friends, today was the best! Through your kindness, respect and teamwork, you have once again made our town a clean, safe and happy place.

And now for some big news of my own!

Tomorrow at dawn, I'll be heading out for a few weeks in search of new stories from far away places. I know I'm leaving Peaceville in good hands, paws and claws. When I return from my adventures, I shall report what I've heard, seen and smelled with all of you. Till then, keep my seat warm!"

Next morning at sunrise, Lola's pals gathered at her dog house to send her off.

The crows cawed,
"Hurry back please!"

The raccoons chimed in,
"Keep your paws on top of everything Lola."

The dogs woofed,
"Be careful who you smell!"

The bunny whispered,
"Where's Lola going?"

Farmer Rabbit answered,
"Wherever she can be a helper."

As Lola trotted out of town, she waved
her paw and barked, "Bye my good
pals. Keep up the good work!"

They happily shouted back,
"You can count on us Lola!"

"We're all in this together!"

What kind of stories will Lola bring
back to Peaceville?

Stay tuned. "Woof!"

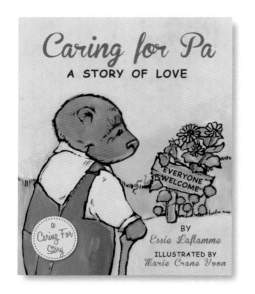

Caring for Pa
A STORY OF LOVE

EVERYONE WELCOME

BY
Essie Laflamme

ILLUSTRATED BY
Marie Crane Yvon

a Caring For Story

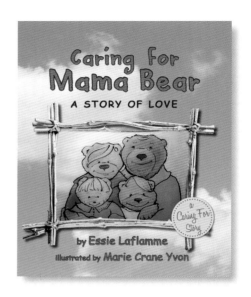

Caring for Mama Bear
A STORY OF LOVE

by Essie Laflamme

illustrated by Marie Crane Yvon

a Caring For Story

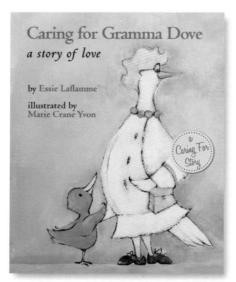

Caring for Gramma Dove
a story of love

by Essie Laflamme

illustrated by
Marie Crane Yvon

a Caring For Story

The Caring For Series
SWEET ECHO STORIES

"We are ALL in this together."

about the
"Caring For"
series of books

The "Caring For" stories are in honor of every child and family that Essie has had the immense privilege to care for and become friends with through palliative and hospice service. These gentle and comforting books are a compilation of beautiful memories from each home into which she was welcomed - the children are the heroes behind each story. Essie believes, "Everyone deserves to write the last chapter of their life." These are their stories.

about the
"Lola, The Roving Reporter"
series of books

In addition to writing tender bereavement books, Essie also writes playful and light-hearted stories as seen through the eyes of canine confidente, Lola, and her zany cast of characters. Lola's humorous adventures are sweetly sprinkled with palpable, meaningful and tangible messages of respect and empathy that are gently conveyed through scenarios that children of all ages will relate to.

And, as always, the center of this Sweet Echo Series is the heart.

To learn more please visit:
sweetechostories.com

AUTHOR
ESSIE LAFLAMME

Essie Laflamme, author of "Lola, the Roving Reporter" and the "Caring For" series, is an experienced preschool teacher, palliative care and hospice volunteer who has always used the charm of puppetry in the caring of children. Essie called Lola her therapy dog and best friend. Lola often 'wagged along' with Essie into class-rooms, homes and hospitals. Through their journey she began writing light- hearted stories with tender-hearted messages about her pal Lola. Essie resides in Granby, MA and Santa Barbara, CA.

ILLUSTRATOR
MARIE CRANE YVON

Marie Crane Yvon is a professional decorative artist and designer. The first day Marie's family brought their new puppy home, Essie and Lola were the very first friends to visit! Pals Lola and Teddy inspired the creative artistry behind this story of friendship and community. Marie resides in the valley of Western MA.

FOR MORE INFORMATION
PLEASE VISIT OUR WEBSITE:

sweetechostories.com